The New Kid on the Block

The New Kid

The New Kid on the Block

on the Block

poems by JACK PRELUTSKY
drawings by JAMES STEVENSON

MAMMOTH

First published in Great Britain 1986
by William Heinemann Ltd
Published 1991 by Mammoth
an imprint of Reed International Books Ltd
Michelin House, 81 Fulham Road, London SW3 6RB
and Auckland, Melbourne, Singapore and Toronto

Reprinted 1991, 1992, 1996

Text copyright © 1984 by Jack Prelutsky
Illustrations copyright © 1984 by James Stevenson

ISBN 0 7497 0602 3

A CIP catalogue record for this title
is available from the British Library

Printed and bound in Great Britain
by Cox & Wyman Ltd, Reading, Berkshire

For Susan Hirschman
—20 years—

The New Kid on the Block

There's a new kid on the block,
and boy, that kid is tough,
that new kid punches hard,
that new kid plays real rough,
that new kid's big and strong,
with muscles everywhere,
that new kid tweaked my arm,
that new kid pulled my hair.

That new kid likes to fight,
and picks on all the guys,
that new kid scares me some,
(that new kid's twice my size),
that new kid stomped my toes,
that new kid swiped my ball,
that new kid's really bad,
I don't care for her at all.

Jellyfish Stew

Jellyfish stew,
I'm loony for you,
I dearly adore you,
oh, truly I do,
you're creepy to see,
revolting to chew,
you slide down inside
with a hullabaloo.

You're soggy, you're smelly,
you taste like shampoo,
you bog down my belly
with oodles of goo,
yet I would glue noodles
and prunes to my shoe,
for one oozy spoonful
of jellyfish stew.

Nine Mice

Nine mice on tiny tricycles
went riding on the ice,
they rode in spite of warning signs,
they rode despite advice.

The signs were right, the ice was thin,
in half a trice, the mice fell in,
and from their chins down to their toes,
those mice entirely froze.

Nine mindless mice, who paid the price,
are thawing slowly by the ice,
still sitting on their tricycles
. . . nine white and shiny *micicles!*

Clara Cleech

The poorest juggler ever seen
was clumsy Clara Cleech,
who juggled a bean, a nectarine,
a pumpkin, and a peach.

She juggled a stone, a slide trombone,
a celery stalk, a stick,
a seeded roll, a salad bowl,
a bagel, a boot, a brick.

With relative ease she juggled a cheese,
she juggled a lock, a lime,
yes, Clara juggled all of these
. . . *but just one at a time.*

I Wonder Why Dad Is So Thoroughly Mad

I wonder why Dad is so thoroughly mad,
I can't understand it at all,
unless it's the bee still afloat in his tea,
or his underwear, pinned to the wall.

Perhaps it's the dye on his favorite tie,
or the mousetrap that snapped in his shoe,
or the pipeful of gum that he found with his thumb,
or the toilet, sealed tightly with glue.

It can't be the bread crumbled up in his bed,
or the slugs someone left in the hall,
I wonder why Dad is so thoroughly mad,
I can't understand it at all.

Drumpp the Grump

I'm Drumpp, the grump of the garbage dump,
I'm a contradictory cuss,
I'm grubby and gruff, and just as rough
as an old rhinoceros.

I never wash, and like to squash
my fingers into worms,
I'm full of fleas and smelly cheese
and fifty million germs.

I swallow food before it's chewed,
I belch an awful lot,
I smell like a goat, and wear a coat
that swarms with slime and rot.

I'm mean as a bear that's burned his hair,
I've nothing nice to say,
I don't like you . . . or *you* . . . or YOU!
You'd better go away.

I'm Drumpp, the grump of the garbage dump,
I'm hard as a battering ram,
but I want you to know before you go . . .
I LIKE THE WAY I AM!

Alligators Are Unfriendly

Alligators are unfriendly,
they are easily upset,
I suspect that I would never
care to have one for a pet.
Oh, I know they do not bellow,
and I think they do not shed,
but I'd probably be nervous
if I had one in my bed.

Alligators are not clever,
they are something of a bore,
they can't heel or catch a Frisbee,
they don't greet you at the door,
for their courtesy is lacking,
and their tempers are not sweet,
they won't even fetch your slippers
. . . though they just might eat your feet.

You Need to Have an Iron Rear

You need to have an iron rear
to sit upon a cactus,
or otherwise, at least a year
of very painful practice.

The Underwater Wibbles

The Underwater Wibbles
dine exclusively on cheese,
they keep it in containers
which they bind about their knees,
they often chew on Cheddar
which they slice into a dish,
and gorge on Gorgonzola
to the wonder of the fish.

The Underwater Wibbles
wiggle blithely through the sea,
munching merrily on Muenster,
grated Feta, bits of Brie,
passing porpoises seem puzzled,
stolid octopuses stare,
as the Wibbles nibble Gouda,
Provolone, Camembert.

The Underwater Wibbles
frolic gaily off the coast,
eating melted Mozzarella
served on soggy crusts of toast,
Wibbles gobble Appenzeller
as they execute their dives,
oh, the Underwater Wibbles
live extraordinary lives.

I Am Running in a Circle

I am running in a circle
and my feet are getting sore,
and my head is
spinning
spinning
as it's never spun before,
I am
dizzy
dizzy
dizzy.
Oh! I cannot bear much more,
I am trapped in a
revolving
. . . volving
. . . volving
. . . volving door!

Cuckoo!

The cuckoo in our cuckoo clock
was wedded to an octopus,
she laid a single wooden egg,
and hatched a cuckoocloctopus.

Do Oysters Sneeze?

Do oysters sneeze beneath the seas,
or wiggle to and fro,
or sulk, or smile, or dance awhile
. . . how can we ever know?

Do oysters yawn when roused at dawn,
and do they ever weep,
and can we tell, when, in its shell,
an oyster is asleep?

Mabel, Remarkable Mabel

Oh, Mabel, remarkable Mabel,
your dining demeanor is queer,
you eat with your feet on the table,
while a teaspoon sticks out of your ear.

Your mouth opens wide and then wider,
as you shovel six hamburgers in,
your elbows are dripping with cider,
there is mustard all over your chin.

In your lap lies a lump of linguine,
your toes cling to slices of bread,
your knees balance pounds of zucchini,
there's a pudding on top of your head.

Your nose is spread thickly with butter,
your shoulders hold pickles in brine.
Oh, Mabel, you may make me mutter,
but it's wonderful watching you dine.

Its Fangs Were Red

Its fangs were red with bloody gore,
its eyes were red with menace,
it battered down my bedroom door,
and burst across my bedroom floor,
and with a loud, resounding roar
said, *"ANYONE FOR TENNIS?"*

<u>An Unassuming Owl</u>

An unassuming owl,
having little else to do,
remarked within the darkness
a discreet and subtle "WHOOOOOOOOOOOO!"

A self-important owl,
puffed and pompous in the gloom,
responded with an overblown
and condescending
"WHOOOOOOOOOOOOOOOOOOOOOOO
OOOOOOOOOOOM!"

I've Got an Itch

I've got an itch, a wretched itch,
no other itch could match it,
it itches in the one spot which
I cannot reach, to scratch it.

Snillies

In the middle of a lily,
if you're fortunate, you'll find
little Snillies, dim and silly,
not a one has any mind.

Snillies move in mass confusion,
hopping here and skipping there,
yet they reach no firm conclusion,
though at times they stop and stare.

Snillies fail to eat their dinner,
Snillies let their lunch slip by,
every day they're growing thinner,
yet they can't imagine why.

Euphonica Jarre

Euphonica Jarre has a voice that's bizarre,
but Euphonica warbles all day,
as windowpanes shatter and chefs spoil the batter
and mannequins moan with dismay.

Mighty ships run aground at her horrible sound,
pretty pictures fall out of their frames,
trees drop off their branches,
rocks start avalanches,
and flower beds burst into flames.

When she opens her mouth, even eagles head south,
little fish truly wish they could drown,
the buzzards all hover, as tigers take cover,
and rats pack their bags and leave town.

Milk turns into butter and butterflies mutter
and bees look for something to sting,
pigs peel off their skins, a tornado begins
when Euphonica Jarre starts to sing.

I'm Thankful

I'm thankful for my baseball bat,
I cracked it yesterday,
I'm thankful for my checker set,
I haven't learned to play,
I'm thankful for my mittens,
one is missing in the snow,
I'm thankful for my hamsters,
they escaped a month ago.

I'm thankful for my basketball,
it's sprung another leak,
I'm thankful for my parakeet,
it bit me twice last week,
I'm thankful for my bicycle,
I crashed into a tree,
I'm thankful for my roller skates,
I fell and scraped my knee.

I'm thankful for my model plane,
it's short a dozen parts,
I'm thankful for my target game,
I'm sure I'll find the darts,
I'm thankful for my bathing suit,
it came off in the river,
I'm thankful for so many things,
except, of course, for LIVER!

A Wolf Is at the Laundromat

A wolf is at the Laundromat,
it's not a wary stare-wolf,
it's short and fat, it tips its hat,
unlike a scary glare-wolf.

It combs its hair, it clips its toes,
it is a fairly rare wolf,
that's only there to clean its clothes—
it is a wash–and–wear–wolf.

No, I *Won't* Turn Orange!

No, I *won't* turn orange
if I eat this orange,
so don't you give me that!
No, I *won't* turn orange
if I eat this orange,
you're talking through your hat!

No, I *won't* turn orange
if I eat this orange,
that's just a bunch of stuff!
No, I *won't* turn orange
if I eat this orange,
I'm going to call your bluff!

No, I *won't* turn orange
if I eat this orange,
so who are you trying to kid?
No, I *won't* turn orange
if I eat this orange. . . .
Well, what do you know,
I DID!

Granny Grizer

Granny Grizer, greedy miser,
is immeasurably mean,
if she sees that you are hungry,
she won't offer you a bean,
she's so absolutely selfish,
she'd deny a dog a bone,
if she owned a million mountains,
no one else would have a stone.

She would charge you for her shadow,
she would charge you for a splinter,
she would charge you for a snowflake
in the middle of the winter,
for she clings to every nickel,
every button, every crumb,
Granny Grizer, greedy miser,
is as stingy as they come.

The Neighbors Are Not Fond of Me

The neighbors are not fond of me,
I've little doubt of that,
for when I near their door, I see
they hide the WELCOME mat.

Ah! A Monster's Lot Is Merry

Ah! A monster's lot is merry
in the melancholy swamp,
here I'm free to be offensive,
free to frolic, free to romp,
what a lark it is to muddle
in the middle of the murk,
making nauseating noises,
driving birds a bit berserk.

There is nothing quite so pleasant
as a solitary trudge
through the wretched desolation
of the pestilential sludge,
how divine to wade and wallow,
and I find I never tire
of distressing little fishes
as I dive beneath the mire.

It's despicably delicious
to disport about the bogs,
making disconcerting faces,
discombobulating frogs,
I consider, as I slither
through an endless sea of slime,
that a monster's lot is merry,
so I'm merry all the time.

Louder than a Clap of Thunder!

Louder than a clap of thunder,
louder than an eagle screams,
louder than a dragon blunders,
or a dozen football teams,
louder than a four-alarmer,
or a rushing waterfall,
louder than a knight in armor
jumping from a ten-foot wall.

Louder than an earthquake rumbles,
louder than a tidal wave,
louder than an ogre grumbles
as he stumbles through his cave,
louder than stampeding cattle,
louder than a cannon roars,
louder than a giant's rattle,
that's how loud my father *SNORES!*

The Bloders Are Exploding

The Bloders are exploding,
they are bursting left and right,
like vials of nitroglycerine,
or sticks of dynamite.

They are going up like rockets,
they are popping here and there,
the sky is filled with Bloders
detonating in the air.

There's a simple explanation
for this odd catastrophe,
you are bound to go to pieces
when you dine on TNT.

Sneaky Sue

I am standing by this lamppost
on the watch for Sneaky Sue,
if I do not see her shortly,
we are finished, we are through,
our private game of hide-and-seek
began a month ago,
so far I haven't found her,
though I've hunted high and low.

I started out by scouting
every building on the block,
I checked inside our clubhouse,
and behind her special rock,
I rummaged through the bushes,
but I couldn't find a clue,
I climbed a tree for nothing—
not a sign of Sneaky Sue.

I covered every corner
of the lot where little grows,
I peered into the garbage cans
and had to hold my nose,
I searched the haunted cellar
where I'd never been before,
it made me sort of nervous—
I heard murmurs on the floor.

I poked through every alley,
and I peeked in every nook,
I have gotten quite disgusted,
for there's nowhere left to look,
so I'm standing by this lamppost
in our game of hide-and-seek . . .
"Sneaky Sue, come out of hiding,
I will wait just one more week!"

The Carpenter Rages

The carpenter rages, the carpenter rants,
the carpenter raises a clamor,
it's all on account of the carpenter ants,
who have eaten the carpenter's hammer.

The carpenter bellows, the carpenter screams,
the carpenter clenches his jaw,
for the carpenter ants, in well-organized teams,
have eaten the carpenter's saw.

The carpenter sputters, the carpenter stews,
the carpenter simmers and sizzles,
for the carpenter ants, working swiftly in crews,
have eaten the carpenter's chisels.

The carpenter sits in a heap on the ground,
the carpenter grows ever madder,
for the carpenter ants, swarming up and around,
have eaten the carpenter's ladder.

The carpenter suddenly leaps in the air,
he writhes in a furious dance,
for those carpenter ants, with incredible flair,
have eaten the carpenter's pants.

We Heard Wally Wail

We heard Wally wail through the whole
    neighborhood,
as his mother whaled Wally as hard as she could,
she made Wally holler, she made Wally whoop,
for what he had spelled in the alphabet soup.

<u>What Nerve You've Got, Minerva Mott!</u>

What nerve you've got, Minerva Mott!
You're miserable! You're mean!
I'd like to tie you in a knot
and paint your stomach green.

I wish two tigers and a bear
would chase you up a tree.
Minerva Mott! How could you dare
to name your dog for me?

Dainty Dottie Dee

There's no one as immaculate
as dainty Dottie Dee,
who clearly is the cleanest
that a human being can be,
no sooner does she waken
than she hoses down her bed,
then hurries to the kitchen,
and disinfects the bread.

She spends the morning sweeping
every inch of every room,
when all the floors are spotless,
Dottie polishes the broom,
she mops the walls and ceilings,
she scrubs beneath the rug,
and should a bug meander by,
she tidies up that bug.

Dottie boils the phone and toaster,
Dottie rinses the shampoo,
she waxes the salami,
and she vacuums the stew,
she dusts the cheese and crackers,
and she sponges down the pie,
she lathers the spaghetti,
then hangs it up to dry.

Dottie scours the locks and keyholes,
and she soaps the bathroom scale,
she launders every light bulb,
she bathes the morning mail,
but her oddest habit ever
(and of this there's little doubt),
is washing all the garbage
before she throws it out.

I've Got an Incredible Headache

I've got an incredible headache,
my temples are throbbing with pain,
it feels like a freight train with two locomotives
is chugging about in my brain.
I'm sure I can't stand it much longer,
my skull's being squeezed in a vise,
as regiments march to the blaring of trumpets,
and thousands of tap-dancing mice.

My head's filled with horrible noises,
there's a man mashing melons inside,
someone keeps drumming on bongos and plumbing,
as porpoises thrash in the tide.
An elephant herd is stampeding,
a volcano is blowing its top,
and if I keep hitting my head with this hammer,
I doubt that my headache will stop.

Ounce and Bounce

Bowen Ounce and Owen Bounce
fell off a speeding train,
both were rather fortunate,
and lived to fall again.

Owen Bounce, who weighed an ounce,
was cushioned by soft shrubbery,
Bowen Ounce just bounced and bounced,
for he was round and rubbery.

Bleezer's Ice Cream

I am Ebenezer Bleezer,
I run BLEEZER'S ICE CREAM STORE,
there are flavors in my freezer
you have never seen before,
twenty-eight divine creations
too delicious to resist,
why not do yourself a favor,
try the flavors on my list:

COCOA MOCHA MACARONI

TAPIOCA SMOKED BALONEY

CHECKERBERRY CHEDDAR CHEW

CHICKEN CHERRY HONEYDEW

TUTTI-FRUTTI STEWED TOMATO

TUNA TACO BAKED POTATO

LOBSTER LITCHI LIMA BEAN

MOZZARELLA MANGOSTEEN

ALMOND HAM MERINGUE SALAMI

YAM ANCHOVY PRUNE PASTRAMI

SASSAFRAS SOUVLAKI HASH

SUKIYAKI SUCCOTASH

BUTTER BRICKLE PEPPER PICKLE

POMEGRANATE PUMPERNICKEL

PEACH PIMENTO PIZZA PLUM

PEANUT PUMPKIN BUBBLEGUM

BROCCOLI BANANA BLUSTER

CHOCOLATE CHOP SUEY CLUSTER

AVOCADO BRUSSELS SPROUT

PERIWINKLE SAUERKRAUT

COTTON CANDY CARROT CUSTARD

CAULIFLOWER COLA MUSTARD

ONION DUMPLING DOUBLE DIP

TURNIP TRUFFLE TRIPLE FLIP

GARLIC GUMBO GRAVY GUAVA

LENTIL LEMON LIVER LAVA

ORANGE OLIVE BAGEL BEET

WATERMELON WAFFLE WHEAT

I am Ebenezer Bleezer,
I run BLEEZER'S ICE CREAM STORE,
taste a flavor from my freezer,
you will surely ask for more.

Henrietta Snetter

Henrietta Snetter knit a sweater in the night,
in a nutty, neat, and novel sort of way,
for she knit it from the sheep
that she counted in her sleep,
and she wore it when she rose to greet the day.

A Cow's Outside

A cow's outside is mainly hide,
undoubtedly this leather
retains a cow's insides inside,
and holds a cow together.

The Flotz

I am the Flotz, I gobble dots,
indeed, I gobble lots and lots,
every dot I ever see
is bound to be a bite for me.
I often munch on myriads
of sweet, abundant periods,
I nibble hyphens, and with ease
chew succulent apostrophes.

From time to time, I turn my gaze
to little dotted "i's" and "j's,"
and if I chance upon a dash,
I soon dispatch it with panache.
I chomp on commas half the day,
quotation marks are rarer prey,
a semicolon's quite a treat,
while polka dots are joys to eat.

When I confront a dotted line,
my tongue flicks out, those dots are mine,
Morse code becomes a feast, and yes,
I've snacked upon an S.O.S.
For I'm the Flotz, who gobbles dots,
I gobble them in pails and pots,
and you'll not like my brief embrace
if you have freckles on your face.

Homework! Oh, Homework!

Homework! Oh, homework!
I hate you! You stink!
I wish I could wash you
away in the sink,
if only a bomb
would explode you to bits.
Homework! Oh, homework!
You're giving me fits.

I'd rather take baths
with a man-eating shark,
or wrestle a lion
alone in the dark,
eat spinach and liver,
pet ten porcupines,
than tackle the homework
my teacher assigns.

Homework! Oh, homework!
You're last on my list,
I simply can't see
why you even exist,
if you just disappeared
it would tickle me pink.
Homework! Oh, homework!
I hate you! You stink!

Bulgy Bunne

Bulgy Bunne (the wonder builder)
built a boat of brass and wood,
Bulgy chose the finest lumber,
and the brass was just as good.
Every plank he picked was perfect,
there was not a knot in one,
for the best was barely suited
to the boat of Bulgy Bunne.

Bulgy scraped and sawed and sanded,
chiseled, hammered, planed, and drilled,
as he built the grandest sailboat
it was possible to build.
Bulgy buffed and Bulgy burnished,
Bulgy raised a sturdy mast,
Bulgy stitched the strongest fabrics
into sails designed to last.

When his work was finally finished,
Bulgy studied it with pride,
for he knew his stalwart sailboat
was prepared to face the tide.
Bulgy Bunne made but one blunder,
Bulgy's boat will not leave shore,
Bulgy built it in his bedroom
. . . it won't fit through Bulgy's door.

Song of the Gloopy Gloppers

We are Gloppers, gloopy Gloppers,
mucilaginous, gelatinous,
we never fail to find a frail
yet filling form to fatten us,
we ooze about the countryside,
through hamlet and metropolis,
for Gloppers ooze where Gloppers choose,
enveloping the populace.

We are Gloppers, gloopy Gloppers,
unrelenting, irresistible,
what we will do to you is too
distressing to be listable,
we'll ooze into your living room,
your kitchen, and your vestibule,
and in your bed we'll taste your head,
to test if you're digestible.

We are Gloppers, gloopy Gloppers,
globs of undulating Glopper ooze,
you cannot quell our viscid swell,
there is no way to stop our ooze,
for Gloppers are invincible,
unquenchable, unstoppable,
and when we swarm upon *your* form,
we know we'll find you GLOPPABLE!

Stringbean Small

Stringbean Small was tall and trim,
basketball seemed meant for him,
at eight foot four, a coach's dream,
and yet he failed to make the team.

It seems at practice, Stringbean Small
began to chew the basketball,
the coach screamed, "Stop! Don't nibble it!
I wanted you to *dribble* it!"

My Baby Brother

My baby brother is so small,
he hasn't even learned to crawl.
He's only been around a week,
and all he seems to do is bawl
and wiggle, sleep . . . and leak.

My Dog, He Is an Ugly Dog

My dog, he is an ugly dog,
he's put together wrong,
his legs are much too short for him,
his ears are much too long.
My dog, he is a scruffy dog,
he's missing clumps of hair,
his face is quite ridiculous,
his tail is scarcely there.

My dog, he is a dingy dog,
his fur is full of fleas,
he sometimes smells like dirty socks,
he sometimes smells like cheese.
My dog, he is a noisy dog,
he's hardly ever still,
he barks at almost anything,
his voice is loud and shrill.

My dog, he is a stupid dog,
his mind is slow and thick,
he's never learned to catch a ball,
he cannot fetch a stick.
My dog, he is a greedy dog,
he eats enough for three,
his belly bulges to the ground,
he is the dog for me.

Be Glad Your Nose Is on Your Face

Be glad your nose is on your face,
not pasted on some other place,
for if it were where it is not,
you might dislike your nose a lot.

Imagine if your precious nose
were sandwiched in between your toes,
that clearly would not be a treat,
for you'd be forced to smell your feet.

Your nose would be a source of dread
were it attached atop your head,
it soon would drive you to despair,
forever tickled by your hair.

Within your ear, your nose would be
an absolute catastrophe,
for when you were obliged to sneeze,
your brain would rattle from the breeze.

Your nose, instead, through thick and thin,
remains between your eyes and chin,
not pasted on some other place—
be glad your nose is on your face!

Mean Maxine

There's no one mean as mean Maxine,
she smells like old cigars,
her brain is smaller than a bean,
I wish she'd move to Mars.

Some day I'll list the things I hate,
and that is where I'll list her,
I'd like to pack her in a crate—
too bad Maxine's my sister.

We Each Wore Half a Horse

We each wore half a horse,
and pranced in a parade,
and you can guess, of course,
which half of it *I* played.

Yubbazubbies

Yubbazubbies, you are yummy,
you are succulent and sweet,
you are splendidly delicious,
quite delectable to eat,
how I smack my lips with relish
when you bump against my knees,
then nuzzle up beside me,
chirping, "Eat us if you please!"

You are juicy, Yubbazubbies,
you are tender, never tough,
you are appetizing morsels,
I can never get enough,
you have captivating flavors
and a tantalizing smell,
a bit like candied apple,
and a bit like caramel.

Yubbazubbies, you are luscious,
you are soft and smooth as silk,
like a dish of chicken dumplings,
or a glass of chocolate milk,
even when I'm hardly hungry,
I am sure to taste a few,
and I'm never disappointed,
Yubbazubbies, I love you.

Dauntless Dimble

Dauntless Dimble was the bravest
of the bravest of the brave,
Dimble climbed the highest mountain,
he explored the deepest cave,
Dimble fought the fiercest creatures,
but he never met his match,
Dimble often wrestled tigers
and escaped without a scratch.

Not a challenge went unanswered,
he accepted every dare,
Dimble walked on blazing embers
and was none the worse for wear,
Dimble exited an airplane
high above a rocky butte,
he escaped with minor bruises
though he wore no parachute.

Dimble diving in the ocean
was beset by hungry sharks,
yet the only wounds he suffered
were some superficial marks,
once a polar bear attacked him
on the icy arctic floes,
the result of that adventure
was a slightly bloody nose.

Dimble danced with deadly cobras,
Dimble toyed with killer bees,
Dimble dangled by one finger
from a tiny greased trapeze,
but he rose from sleep one morning,
and while getting out of bed,
Dimble tripped upon the carpet,
where he cracked his dauntless head.

I Spied My Shadow Slinking

I spied my shadow slinking
up behind me in the night,
I issued it a challenge,
and we started in to fight.

I wrestled with that shadow,
but it wasn't any fun,
I tried my very hardest—
all the same, my shadow won.

Today Is a Day to Crow About

Today is a day to crow about,
it's a crowable sort of day,
for the crows have frightened the scarecrow,
and the scarecrow is running away.

I Found a Four-Leaf Clover

I found a four-leaf clover
and was happy with my find,
but with time to think it over,
I've entirely changed my mind.
I concealed it in my pocket,
safe inside a paper pad,
soon, much swifter than a rocket,
my good fortune turned to bad.

I smashed my fingers in a door,
I dropped a dozen eggs,
I slipped and tumbled to the floor,
a dog nipped both my legs,
my ring slid down the bathtub drain,
my pen leaked on my shirt,
I barked my shin, I missed my train,
I sat on my dessert.

I broke my brand-new glasses,
and I couldn't find my keys,
I stepped in spilled molasses,
and was stung by angry bees.
When the kitten ripped the curtain,
and the toast burst into flame,
I was absolutely certain
that the clover was to blame.

I buried it discreetly
in the middle of a field,
now my luck has changed completely,
and my wounds have almost healed.
If I ever find another,
I will simply let it be,
or I'll give it to my brother—
he deserves it more than me.

Gussie's Greasy Spoon

Every day, at ten past noon,
I enter GUSSIE'S GREASY SPOON,
I plop down in the nearest seat,
and order food unfit to eat.
I try the juice, it's warm and vile,
the scrambled eggs are green as bile,
the beets are blue, the beans are gray,
the cauliflower tastes like clay.

At GUSSIE'S GREASY SPOON, the stew
is part cement, part hay, part glue,
it's mostly gristle, ropy tough,
a tiger couldn't chew the stuff.
The rancid soup is foul and thin,
a bit like bitter medicine,
the melon smells, the salad sags,
the mashed potatoes seem like rags.

One whiff of Gussie's weird cuisine
makes stomachs ache, turns faces green,
her moldy muffins have no peers,
they'll make you sick for forty years.
The coffee's cold, the cake is stale,
the doughnuts taste like pickled whale,
yet, every day, at ten past noon,
I eat at GUSSIE'S GREASY SPOON.

New York Is in North Carolina

New York is in North Carolina.
Seattle is found in Peru.
New Mexico borders on Norway and Italy.
Boston's near Kalamazoo.
Quebec is a town in Hawaii.
Connecticut lies in Trieste.

Those are a few of the answers I wrote
when I flunked the geography test.

Super-Goopy Glue

Permit me to present to you
my famous SUPER-GOOPY GLUE,
by far the finest glue on earth,
one dollar for a penny's worth.

It's rumored that my glue adheres
for easily a thousand years,
my glue's the glue you surely seek,
it's guaranteed for one whole week.

My SUPER-GOOPY GLUE can glue
a carrot to a caribou,
a feather to a ferret's feet,
a pickle to a parakeet.

No other glue is half as good,
it works on metal, glass, and wood,
I'd demonstrate it for you, but
my glue has glued my gluepot shut.

The Cherries' Garden Gala

The Cherries' garden gala
was the finest seen in years,
the Pears arrived in couples,
and the Prunes all carried shears,
the Greens had splendid collars,
and the Peaches wore new shoes,
an Orange danced a hornpipe,
and a Berry sang the blues.

The Beets were playing bongos,
as the Lettuce marched ahead,
the Zucchini made a racket,
but the Ginger seemed well-bred,
the Dates appeared unsteady,
though the Currants stayed on course,
the Turnips whirled in circles,
and the Radishes grew hoarse.

The Beans could not stop coughing
as the Corn told awful jokes,
the Plums were bobbing gaily
with some hearty Artichokes,
a Cauliflower listened
as the Grapes began to whine,
and the Melons started bawling
just to see the Apples pine.

When the Garlic dropped a penny
and the Mint produced a bill,
the Chard grew overheated,
and a Pepper caught a chill,
then the Rhubarb got to fighting,
and the Lemons seemed afraid,
but the Thyme could not help watching,
though the Mushrooms all sought aid.

The Onions dipped politely,
as the Leeks began to spring,
the Sage repeated maxims,
and the Carrots formed a ring,
a Tomato acted saucy
to a rather bossy Pea,
and Potatoes wept with pleasure
at the Cherries' jubilee.

An Alley Cat with One Life Left

I'm an alley cat with one life left,
I started out with nine,
but lost the first in a knockdown fight
with a cat named Frankenstein,
my second went soon after that
to something that I ate,
my third went under a garbage truck—
I noticed it too late.

While strolling through the zoo one day,
I heard an awful roar,
I'd strayed into a lion's cage—
so much for number four,
I lost my fifth one morning
to a ton of falling bricks,
then tumbled from a window ledge,
and gave up number six.

My seventh went to a Saint Bernard—
I was no match for him,
my eighth was squandered in the lake—
it seems I couldn't swim,
so now I'd better watch my step,
I'm down to number nine,
I'm an alley cat with one life left,
and glad that life is mine.

An Irritating Creature

There's an irritating creature
in my living room today,
it's been here for a year now,
and it will not go away.
The first time that I saw it,
it was in my easy chair,
and displayed no inclination
to forsake its station there.

I put it in a parcel,
and I left it at the store,
the thing was there to greet me
when I opened up my door,
I took it to the forest,
and I tied it to a tree,
I found it in my kitchen
having sandwiches and tea.

I packed it in a carton
to disguise its size and shape,
I wrapped it and I stamped it
and I sealed it shut with tape,
I mailed it to the middle
of a mountain in Tibet,
I returned to see it sitting
on my brand-new TV set.

I concealed it in a rocket
that was bound for outer space,
it was back that very evening
with a smile upon its face.
It appears I can't evict it,
though I truly wish I could,
it's entirely too tenacious—
I suspect it's here for good.

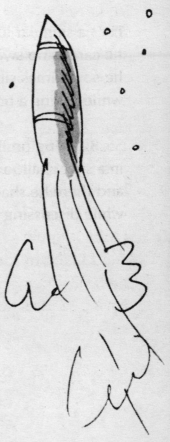

Sir Blushington Bloone

Sir Blushington Bloone is a knight of the court,
with a face like a prune of the large, wrinkled sort,
he's a very odd bird, with a mind of his own,
who is frequently heard singing songs to a stone.

He's a singular lord, with a singular head,
he carries no sword, but a yo-yo instead,
he sometimes sips soup from a small, slotted spoon,
while rolling a hoop to a baffled raccoon.

Sir Blushington Bloone often goes for a ride
in a silver balloon, with a pig by his side,
and there he shampoos his immaculate wig,
while discussing the news of the day with the pig.

By the light of the moon, wearing little or less,
he sits with a loon for an evening of chess,
or waves his baton as he slogs through the bogs,
conducting a swan and a chorus of frogs.

He's been seen on the green on the tips of his toes
as he balances beans on the end of his nose,
he flies kites from his ears every Tuesday at noon,
oh, a knight with no peers is Sir Blushington Bloone.

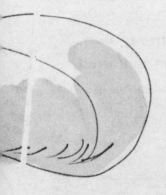

When Tillie Ate the Chili

When Tillie ate the chili,
she erupted from her seat,
she gulped a quart of water,
and fled screaming down the street,
she coughed, she wheezed, she sputtered,
she ran totally amok,
she set a new world record
as she raced around the block.

Tillie's mouth was full of fire,
Tillie's eyes were red with tears,
she was smoking from her nostrils,
she was steaming from her ears,
she cooled off an hour later,
showing perfect self-control
as she said, "What tasty chili,
I should like another bowl."

Never Mince Words with a Shark

You may quarrel with centipedes, quibble with seals,
declaim to a duck in the park,
engage in disputes with cantankerous coots,
but never mince words with a shark.

You may rant at an anteater, banter with eels,
and haggle with gaggles of geese,
heap verbal abuse on a monkey or moose,
but a shark you had best leave in peace.

You may argue with otters, make speeches to teals,
and lecture at length to a shrew,
but a shark will deflate your attempts at debate,
and before you are done, you are through.

I Am Flying!

I am flying! I am flying!
I am riding on the breeze,
I am soaring over meadows,
I am sailing over seas,
I ascend above the cities
where the people, small as ants,
cannot sense the keen precision
of my aerobatic dance.

I am flying! I am flying!
I am climbing unconfined,
I am swifter than the falcon,
and I leave the wind behind,
I am swooping, I am swirling
in a jubilant display,
I am brilliant as a comet
blazing through the Milky Way.

I am flying! I am flying!
I am higher than the moon,
still, I think I'd best be landing,
and it cannot be too soon,
for some nasty information
has lit up my little brain—
I am flying! I am flying!
but I fly without a plane.

The Mungle and the Munn

The duo met to duel at dawn
(the Mungle and the Munn),
to settle certain matters,
as indeed they'd often done.
The Munn struck first and tweaked a cheek,
but being tweaked right back,
detached the Mungle's tender tail,
and dropped it in a sack.

The Mungle dashed his mallet
on his foe's defenseless toes,
the Munn produced his pliers
and removed his rival's nose.
The Mungle, somewhat angered,
gnawed his adversary's ear,
the Munn undid the Mungle's horn,
the Mungle shed a tear.

The contest grew intenser,
and the Mungle, seeing red,
took soap and blade and neatly shaved
the Munn's unguarded head.
They struggled for position,
they attacked with perfect aim,
whatever deed the Mungle did,
the Munn did much the same.

They battled on with cantaloupes,
with sandwiches and snips,
with kegs of pegs, with rotten eggs,
with prunes and paper clips.
At noon the duelists drew apart
(the Mungle and the Munn),
they bowed and said, "Let's meet again—
it's certainly been fun!"

Throckmorton Thratte

Throckmorton Thratte has charm and class,
he's wealthy and he's handsome,
small wonder that his looking glass
is holding him for ransom.

Uncanny Colleen

Uncanny Colleen (unaccountably green)
is munching on cabbage and squash,
while spinning around in her washing machine—
no doubt she'll come out in the wash.

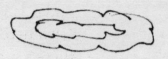

Today Is Very Boring

Today is very boring,
it's a very boring day,
there is nothing much to look at,
there is nothing much to say,
there's a peacock on my sneakers,
there's a penguin on my head,
there's a dormouse on my doorstep,
I am going back to bed.

Today is very boring,
I can hardly help but yawn,
there's a flying saucer landing
in the middle of my lawn,
a volcano just erupted
less than half a mile away,
and I think I felt an earthquake,
it's a very boring day.

Today is very boring,
it is boring through and through,
there is absolutely nothing
that I think I want to do,
I see giants riding rhinos,
and an ogre with a sword,
there's a dragon blowing smoke rings,
I am positively bored.

Griselda Gratz

Griselda Gratz kept sixty cats,
she fed them very well
on angel cakes and raisin flakes
and acorns in a shell.

Her furry crowd patrolled, meowed
about her tiny house,
Griselda Gratz kept sixty cats,
to catch a single mouse.

I Toss Them to My Elephant

When the summer sun is blazing,
I pick daisy after daisy,
I toss them to my elephant—
it makes him slightly crazy.

I gather up chrysanthemums
when fall is in the air,
I toss them to my elephant—
it makes him stand and stare.

I harvest bright poinsettias
in winter, when it's chilly,
I toss them to my elephant—
it makes him sort of silly.

I pluck bouquets of tulips
when they blossom in the spring,
I toss them to my elephant . . .
it always makes him sing!

A Microscopic Topic

I am a paramecium
that cannot do a simple sum,
and it's a rather well-known fact
I'm quite unable to subtract.

If I'd an eye, I'd surely cry
about the way I multiply,
for though I've often tried and tried,
I do it backward . . . and divide.

My Brother's Head Should Be Replaced

My brother's head should be replaced,
it's lighter than a feather,
he's trying to use tomato paste
to paste tomatoes together.

Michael Built a Bicycle

Michael built a bicycle
unsuitable for speed,
it's crammed with more accessories
than anyone could need,
there's an AM-FM radio,
a deck to play cassettes,
a refrigerator-freezer,
and a pair of TV sets.

There are shelves for shirts and sweaters,
there are hangers for his jeans,
a drawer for socks and underwear,
a rack for magazines,
there's a fishtank and a birdcage
perched upon the handlebars,
a bookcase, and a telescope
to watch the moon and stars.

There's a telephone, a blender,
and a stove to cook his meals,
there's a sink to do the dishes
somehow fastened to the wheels,
there's a portable piano,
and a set of model trains,
an automatic bumbershoot
that opens when it rains.

There's a desk for typing letters
on his fabulous machine,
a stall for taking showers,
and a broom to keep things clean,
but you'll never see him ride it,
for it isn't quite complete,
Michael left no room for pedals,
and there isn't any seat.

Eggs!

Eggs!
You're excellent, exquisite,
I exalt you, hot or cold,
I salute you in a salad,
I commend you in a mold,
you are scrumptious lightly scrambled,
fully fascinating fried,
incandescent over easy,
dazzling on your sunny side.

Eggs!
You're dainty when you're coddled,
when you're stuffed, I long to bite,
you're angelic when you're deviled,
when you're shirred, you're sheer delight,
you are magic on a muffin,
gold ambrosia on a bun,
you are princely, poached precisely,
when your yellow starts to run.

Eggs!
You're nectar in an omelette,
in soufflés, a savory dream,
baked or boiled you are bewitching,
in a quiche, you reign supreme,
yes, I love you to distraction,
but alas, you have a flaw,
for you're thoroughly revolting
when you're swallowed whole and raw.

The Flimsy Fleek

The flimsy Fleek is mild and meek,
its teeth are dull, its jaws are weak,
it has a fragile, frail physique,
its limbs are lean and little.
Its neck is short, its face is pale,
its lips are thin, its breath is stale,
it has a twist of tufted tail,
its bones are bent and brittle.

It lives beneath a bumbershoot,
it nibbles twigs and bits of fruit,
it only wears its birthday suit,
its skin is thick with wrinkles.
Its ears resemble dinner rolls,
its nose is but two buttonholes,
its eyes are large as salad bowls,
they teem with tiny twinkles.

The Fleek is quite content to dwell
within its share of shady dell,
attempting to subtract and spell,
it is, I fear, not clever.
If you should find this flimsy Fleek,
and are so foolish as to speak,
the Fleek will squeak, and in a streak,
will disappear forever.

Floradora Doe

Consider the calamity
of Floradora Doe,
who talked to all her plants, because
she thought it helped them grow,
she recited to her ivy,
to her fennel, ferns, and phlox,
she chatted with her cacti
in their little window box.

She murmured to her mosses,
and she yammered to her yew,
she babbled to her basil,
to her borage and bamboo,
she lectured to her laurels,
to her lilac and her lime,
she whispered to her willows,
and she tittered to her thyme.

She gossiped with a poppy,
and she prattled to a rose,
she regaled her rhododendrons
with a constant stream of prose,
then suddenly, one morning,
every plant keeled over, dead.
"Alas!" moaned Floradora.
"Was it something that I said?"

Oh, Teddy Bear

Oh, Teddy Bear, dear Teddy,
though you're gone these many years,
I recall with deep affection
how I nibbled on your ears,
I can hardly keep from smiling,
and my heart beats fast and glows,
when I think about the morning
that I twisted off your nose.

Teddy Bear, you didn't whimper,
Teddy Bear, you didn't pout,
when I reached in with my fingers
and I tore your tummy out,
and you didn't even mumble
or emit the faintest cries,
when I pulled your little paws off,
when I bit your button eyes.

Yes, you sat beside me calmly,
and you didn't once protest,
when I ripped apart the stuffing
that was packed inside your chest,
and you didn't seem to notice
when I yanked out all your hair—
it's been ages since I've seen you,
but I miss you, Teddy Bear.

My Mother Says I'm Sickening

My mother says I'm sickening,
my mother says I'm crude,
she says this when she sees me
playing Ping-Pong with my food,
she doesn't seem to like it
when I slurp my bowl of stew,
and now she's got a list of things
she says I mustn't do—

DO NOT CATAPULT THE CARROTS!

DO NOT JUGGLE GOBS OF FAT!

DO NOT DROP THE MASHED POTATOES

ON THE GERBIL OR THE CAT!

NEVER PUNCH THE PUMPKIN PUDDING!

NEVER TUNNEL THROUGH THE BREAD!

PUT NO PEAS INTO YOUR POCKET!

PLACE NO NOODLES ON YOUR HEAD!

DO NOT SQUEEZE THE STEAMED ZUCCHINI!

DO NOT MAKE THE MELON OOZE!

NEVER STUFF VANILLA YOGURT

IN YOUR LITTLE SISTER'S SHOES!

DRAW NO FACES IN THE KETCHUP!

MAKE NO LITTLE GRAVY POOLS!

I wish my mother wouldn't make
so many useless rules.

When Dracula Went to the Blood Bank

When Dracula went to the blood bank,
he thoroughly flustered the staff,
for rather than make a donation,
he drew out a pint and a half.

When Young, the Slyne

When young, the Slyne, from noon to nine,
stood blithely on its head,
and rudely chewed on thread and twine,
"How odd!" I often said.

The Slyne, now grown, chews yet on thread
and twine, from noon to nine,
but does not stand upon its head,
it stands, instead, on mine.

Ballad of a Boneless Chicken

I'm a basic boneless chicken,
yes, I have no bones inside,
I'm without a trace of rib cage,
yet I hold myself with pride,
other hens appear offended
by my total lack of bones,
they discuss me impolitely
in derogatory tones.

I am absolutely boneless,
I am boneless through and through,
I have neither neck nor thighbones,
and my back is boneless too,
and I haven't got a wishbone,
not a bone within my breast,
so I rarely care to travel
from the comfort of my nest.

I have feathers fine and fluffy,
I have lovely little wings,
but I lack the superstructure
to support these splendid things.
Since a chicken finds it tricky
to parade on boneless legs,
I stick closely to the hen house,
laying little scrambled eggs.

Seymour Snorkke

"With chopsticks did I sip my soup,"
so stated Seymour Snorkke,
"but that was much too difficult,
so now I use a fork."

There Is a Thing

There is a thing
beneath the stair
with slimy face
and oily hair
that does not move
or speak or sing
or do another
single thing
but sit and wait
beneath the stair
with slimy face
and oily hair.

Ma! Don't Throw That Shirt Out

Ma! Don't throw that shirt out,
it's my all-time favorite shirt!
I admit it smells peculiar,
and is stained with grease and dirt,
that it's missing half its buttons,
and has got so many holes
that it might have been infested
by a regiment of moles.

Yes! I know that I've outgrown it,
that it's faded and it's torn,
I can see the sleeves are frazzled,
I'm aware the collar's worn,
but I've had that shirt forever,
and I swear that I'll be hurt
if you dare to throw that shirt out—
IT'S MY ALL-TIME FAVORITE SHIRT!

Suzanna Socked Me Sunday

Suzanna socked me Sunday,
she socked me Monday, too,
she also socked me Tuesday,
I was turning black and blue.

She socked me double Wednesday,
and Thursday even more,
but when she socked me Friday,
she began to get me sore.

"Enough's enough," I yelled at her,
"I hate it when you hit me!"
"Well, then I won't!" Suzanna said—
that Saturday, she bit me.

The Zoosher

Beneath a bush, the Zoosher lies,
with mashed potatoes on its eyes,
with fried zucchini in its nose,
with carrot sticks between its toes.
Impaled upon its single horn
are toasted ears of baby corn,
and on its chest, it wears no less
than rhubarb, ringed with watercress.

The Zoosher keeps in either paw
a pair of leeks, one cooked, one raw,
an eggplant dangles from its beard
(some find this practice rather weird).
Assembled neatly on its knees
are little pods of early peas,
while resting boldly on its thighs
are yams of more than average size.

It's hard to fault the Zoosher's taste
(a mushroom belt adorns its waist),
and gaily wrapped about its head
are radishes—some white, some red.
Just why the beast behaves this way
is rather difficult to say,
as here beneath a bush it lies,
with mashed potatoes on its eyes.

I'd Never Eat a Beet

I'd never eat a beet, because
I could not stand the taste,
I'd rather nibble drinking straws,
or fountain pens, or paste,
I'd eat a window curtain
and perhaps a roller skate,
but a beet, you may be certain
would be wasted on my plate.

I would sooner chew on candles
or the laces from my shoes,
or a dozen suitcase handles
were I ever forced to choose,
I would eat a Ping-Pong paddle,
I would eat a Ping-Pong ball,
I might even eat a saddle,
but a beet? No! Not at all.

I would swallow talcum powder
and my little rubber duck,
I'd have doorknobs in my chowder,
I would eat a hockey puck,
I would eat my model rocket
and the socks right off my feet,
I would even eat my pocket,
but I'd never eat a beet!

Boing! Boing! Squeak!

Boing! Boing! Squeak!
Boing! Boing! Squeak!
A bouncing mouse is in my house,
it's been here for a week.

It bounced from out of nowhere,
then quickly settled in,
I'm grateful that it came alone
(I've heard it has a twin),
it bounces in the kitchen,
it bounces in the den,
it bounces through the living room—
look! There it goes again.

Boing! Boing! Squeak!
Boing! Boing! Squeak!
A bouncing mouse is in my house,
it's been here for a week.

It bounces on the sofa,
on the table and the bed,
up the stairs and on the chairs
and even on my head,
that mouse continues bouncing
every minute of the day,
it bounces, bounces, bounces,
but it doesn't bounce away.

Boing! Boing! Squeak!
Boing! Boing! Squeak!
A bouncing mouse is in my house,
it's been here for a week.

I'm Disgusted with My Brother

I'm disgusted with my brother,
I am positively sore,
I have never been so angry
with a human being before,
he's everything detestable
that's spelled with A through Z,
he deserves to be the target
of a ten-pound bumblebee.

I'd like to wave a magic wand
and make him disappear,
or watch a wild rhinoceros
attack him from the rear,
perhaps I'll cook a pot of soup
and dump my brother in,
he forgot today's my birthday—
oh, how could he . . . he's my *twin!*

Dora Diller

"My stomach's full of butterflies!"
lamented Dora Diller.
Her mother sighed. "That's no surprise,
you ate a caterpillar!"

Lavinia Nink

Lavinia Nink lives serenely
in a house unmistakably rare,
for the water turns on in the shower
when Lavinia sits in a chair,
when she opens the door to the freezer,
the clock strikes a quarter to ten,
and as soon as she starts up the oven,
the telephone rings in the den.

When Lavinia plays the piano,
the toaster repeatedly pops,
and the TV keeps changing the channel
whenever Lavinia mops,
all the lights in the living room flicker
when she washes her hands in the sink,
it's a house to drive anyone nutty,
but it's home to Lavinia Nink.

I Do Not Like the Rat!

I praise the hippopotamus,
I celebrate the bat,
I hold the bream in high esteem—
I DO NOT LIKE THE RAT!

I cotton to the octopus,
I tolerate the gnat,
I dote upon the stately swan—
I SHUDDER AT THE RAT!

I value the rhinoceros,
I venerate the cat,
I quite salute the simple newt—
I CANNOT STAND THE RAT!

The Diatonic Dittymunch

The Diatonic Dittymunch
plucked music from the air,
it swallowed scores of symphonies,
and still had space to spare,
sonatas and cantatas
slithered sweetly down its throat,
it made ballads into salads,
and consumed them note by note.

It ate marches and mazurkas,
it ate rhapsodies and reels,
minuets and tarantellas
were the staples of its meals,
but the Diatonic Dittymunch
outdid itself one day,
it ate a three-act opera,
and loudly passed away.

132

I'm Bold, I'm Brave

I'm bold, I'm brave, I know no fear.
I'm gallant as a buccaneer.
Is that a hornet by my ear?
Gangway! I'm getting out of here!

Baloney Belly Billy

Baloney Belly Billy
swallows anything for cash,
if you offer him a penny,
he'll chew paper from the trash,
he'll eat guppies for a nickel,
for a dime, he'll eat a bug,
and a quarter will convince him
that he ought to eat a slug.

I have seen him eat a button,
I have seen him eat a bee,
I have seen him eat three beetles
for a half a dollar fee,
for a dollar he will gladly
eat a lizard off a fence,
just imagine what he'd swallow
for another fifty cents.

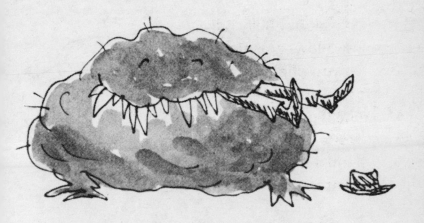

Come See the Thing

Come see the thing that Dad has caught—
oh, yuck! . . . don't even bother,
it is not dead as Dad had thought,
and we are minus Father.

The Nothing-Doings

Meet the lazy Nothing-Doings,
all they do is stand around,
when it's time for doing nothing,
Nothing-Doings can be found,
when it's time for doing something,
you won't find a single one,
for the Nothing-Doings vanish
when there's work that must be done.

I'm the Single Most Wonderful Person I Know

I'm the single most wonderful person I know,
I'm witty, I'm charming, I'm smart,
I'm often so brilliant I actually glow,
I'm a genius in music and art.

I'm super, I'm splendid, I'm stunning, I'm strong,
I'm awesome, I'm dashing, I'm bold,
I know all the answers, it's rare that I'm wrong,
I'm an absolute joy to behold.

I'm strikingly handsome, I'm thoroughly grand,
I'm uncategorically clever,
there's only one thing that I can't understand—
why nobody likes me . . . not ever!

My Sister Is a Sissy

My sister is a sissy,
she's afraid of dogs and cats,
a toad can give her tantrums,
and she's terrified of rats,
she screams at things with stingers,
things that buzz, and things that crawl,
just the shadow of a spider
sends my sister up the wall.

A lizard makes her shiver,
and a turtle makes her squirm,
she positively cringes
at the prospect of a worm,
she's afraid of things with feathers,
she's afraid of things with fur,
she's scared of almost everything—
how come I'm scared of her?

Miraculous Mortimer

Miraculous Mortimer (Master Magician)
has sawn his assistant in two.
He can't recall how to reverse her condition—
has anyone here any glue?

The Cave Beast Greets a Visitor

Ah! Welcome to my chamber,
do step in and stay awhile,
I so rarely host a stranger
in this humble domicile.
You're unquestionably weary,
and could use a bit of rest,
it's my joy to entertain you
as my dearly honored guest.

Undoubtedly you're thirsty,
sip some liquid from this flask,
you appear to have some queries,
I shall answer all you ask.
The skulls within the corner?
The bones within the bin?
Mere decorative trifles—
they were here when I moved in.

My teeth, you say? My talons?
My mandibular expanse?
Quite the ticket for consuming
tender stems of tiny plants.
This blade you see me sharpen?
Let me set your mind at ease—
I find it indispensable
for slicing bread and cheese.

You say you must be going?
Goodness gracious, why the haste?
Dinner simmers on the fire,
you may find it to your taste.
Whet your palate with a spoonful,
it's a most nutritious stew.
What's that? It lacks in savor?
Then I'll flavor it with **YOU!!!**

I'm in a Rotten Mood!

I'm in a rotten mood today,
a really rotten mood today,
I'm feeling cross,
I'm feeling mean,
I'm jumpy as a jumping bean,
I have an awful attitude—
I'M IN A ROTTEN MOOD!

I'm in a rotten mood today,
a really rotten mood today,
I'm in a snit,
I'm in a stew,
there's nothing that I care to do
but sit all by myself and brood—
I'M IN A ROTTEN MOOD!

I'm in a rotten mood today,
a really rotten mood today,
you'd better stay away from me,
I'm just a lump of misery,
I'm feeling absolutely rude—

I'M IN A ROTTEN MOOD!

Something Silky

Something silky, scarcely there,
ghostly and diaphanous,
stole our socks and underwear,
and had a ghastly laugh on us.

Archie B. McCall

The shrewdest salesman anywhere
is Archie B. McCall,
he's king of selling anything
to anyone at all,
Archie's ways are so persuasive
he's been never known to fail,
he has sold a yak a jacket,
sacks of feathers to a snail.

He has sold a fish a hairbrush,
and a snake a pair of shoes,
peddled Pogo sticks and purses
to a troop of kangaroos,
he has sold a camel earmuffs,
and a trumpet to a moose,
a bikini to a beaver,
an umbrella to a goose.

No one ever turns down Archie,
for when Archie's at his best,
he can sell an eagle glasses,
he can sell a worm a vest,
Archie's simply irresistible,
he's matchless, he's a whiz,
he talked *me* into buying *this*—
I wonder what it is.

I'd Never Dine on Dinosaurs

I'd never dine on dinosaurs,
they can't be good to eat,
for all they've got are lots of bones,
and not a bit of meat.

Forty Performing Bananas

We're FORTY PERFORMING BANANAS,
in bright yellow slippery skins,
our features are rather appealing,
though we've neither shoulders nor chins,
we cha-cha, fandango, and tango,
we kick and we skip and we hop,
while half of us belt out a ballad,
the rest of us spin like a top.

We're FORTY PERFORMING BANANAS,
we mambo, we samba, we waltz,
we dangle and swing from the ceiling,
then turn very slick somersaults,
people drive here in bunches to see us,
our splits earn us worldly renown,
we're FORTY PERFORMING BANANAS,
come see us when you are in town.

Sidney Snickke

Serving supper, Sidney Snickke
played a strange and silly trick.

He inserted jumping beans
in his parents' salad greens.

By dessert, his mom and dad
appeared, to Sidney, hopping mad.

I Am Falling off a Mountain

I am falling off a mountain,
I am plummeting through space,
you may see this does not please me
by the frown upon my face.

As the ground keeps getting nearer,
it's a simple task to tell
that I've got a slight dilemma,
that my day's not going well.

My velocity's increasing,
I am dropping like a stone,
I could do with some assistance,
is there someone I can phone?

Though I'm unafraid of falling,
I am prompted to relate
that the landing has me worried,
and I don't have long to wait.

I am running out of options,
there's just one thing left to try—
in the next eleven seconds,
I have got to learn to fly!

Zany Zapper Zockke

The greatest ace of video space
was zany Zapper Zockke,
for just a single quarter
he could play around the clock.
One day he played a fateful game
of **SUPER SPACE SARDINES,**
he loved to zap those fishy blips
to countless smithereens.

They stormed in strange formations
but he boldly beat them back,
with both his blasters blazing,
Zapper weathered each attack.
They employed bizarre maneuvers,
and they set uncanny traps,
yet they met disintegration
from his lightning counter-zaps.

His hands were swift, his aim was true,
his strategy was keen,
he faced those fish invaders,
and he blew them off the screen.
They seemed to swoop from nowhere,
but he calmly kept his wits,
and with sharp and deadly volleys,
Zapper shattered them to bits.

The machine began to sizzle
as the points began to mount,
he zapped so many space sardines
that even *he* lost count.
Then, in a flash, he vanished,
for he moved at such a pace,
that he spun into a time warp—
Zapper Zockke's in hyperspace!

Happy Birthday, Dear Dragon

There were rumbles of strange jubilation
in a dark, subterranean lair,
for the dragon was having a birthday,
and his colleagues were gathering there.
"HOORAH!" groaned the trolls and the ogres
as they pelted each other with stones.
"HOORAH!" shrieked a sphinx and a griffin,
and the skeletons rattled their bones.

"*HOORAH!*" screamed the queen of the demon
"HOORAH!" boomed a giant. "REJOICE!"
"Hoorah!" piped a tiny hobgoblin
in an almost inaudible voice.
"*HOORAH!*" cackled rapturous witches.
"*Hoorahhhhhh!*" hissed a basilisk too.
Then they howled in cacophonous chorus,
"HAPPY BIRTHDAY,
    DEAR DRAGON,
        TO YOU!"

They whistled, they squawked, they applauded,
as they gleefully brought forth the cake.

"OH, THANK YOU!"

he thundered with pleasure
in a bass that made every ear ache.
Then puffing his chest to the fullest,
and taking deliberate aim,
the dragon huffed once at the candles—

**and
the candles
all burst
into
flame!**

Index to Titles

Index to First Lines

157